D1581710

THE TITANIC

An Interactive History Adventure

by Bob Temple

Consultant:
Karen Kamuda, Vice President
Titanic Historical Society and Titanic Museum
Indian Orchard, Massachusetts

Raintree is an imprint of Capstone Global Library Limited, a company incorporated in England and Wales having its registered office at 7 Pilgrim Street, London, EC4V 6LB – Registered company number: 6695582

www.raintreepublishers.co.uk
myorders@raintreepublishers.co.uk

ISBN 978 1 474 70668 1
19 18 17 16 15
10 9 8 7 6 5 4 3 2 1

Printed and bound in China

British Library Cataloguing in Publication Data
A full catalogue record for this book is available from the British Library.

Photo Credits
The Bridgeman Art Library/Private Collection,/Titanic Farewell to Belfast (oil on canvas), Crossley, Harley (Contemporary Artist), 72; The Bridgeman Art Library/Private Collection,/The Titanic Sinking on 15th April 1912, 1991, Crossley, Harley (Contemporary Artist), 67; The Bridgeman Art Library/The Illustrated London News Picture Library, London, UK/The Reading Room on board the Titanic, 1912 (b/w photo), 15; The Bridgeman Art Library/The Illustrated London News Picture Library, London, UK/The Titanic Sinking, from 'The Sphere', 27th April 1912 (engraving) (b&w photo), Matania, Fortunino (1881–1963), 27; Corbis/Bettmann, 41, 95; Corbis/Hulton-Deutsch Collection, 24; Corbis/Ralph White, cover, 11, 48; Corbis Sygma, 12; Getty Images Inc./Time & Life Pictures, 60; The Granger Collection, New York, 8–9, 93, 100; The Granger Collection, New York/Willy Stöwer–ullstein bild, 37; Library of Congress/George Grantham Bain Collection, 103; Mary Evans Picture Library, 35, 42, 81, 84; North Wind Picture Archives, 20, 69, 97; Rex USA/Stanley Lehrer Collection, 57; Rex USA/Tony Davies, 6; Titanic Historical Society and Titanic Museum, 16, 30, 46, 50, 77, 89

Every effort has been made to contact copyright holders of material reproduced in this book. Any omissions will be rectified in subsequent printings if notice is given to the publisher.

All the internet addresses (URLs) given in this book were valid at the time of going to press. However, due to the dynamic nature of the internet, some addresses may have changed, or sites may have changed or ceased to exist since publication. While the author and publisher regret any inconvenience this may cause readers, no responsibility for any such changes can be accepted by either the author or the publisher.

TABLE OF CONTENTS

About your adventure 5

Chapter 1
All aboard! 7
Chapter 2
A first-class experience 13
Chapter 3
On the way to the United States 47
Chapter 4
To protect and serve 73
Chapter 5
After the disaster 101

Time line 106
Other paths to explore 108
Read more 109
Internet sites 109
Glossary 110
Bibliography 111
Index 112

ABOUT YOUR ADVENTURE

YOU are aboard *Titanic*, the world's largest ocean liner. The ship has hit an iceberg and is headed to the bottom of the sea. Will you survive?

In this book, you'll explore how the choices people made meant the difference between life and death. The events you'll experience happened to real people.

Chapter one sets the scene. Then you choose which path to read. Follow the directions at the bottom of each page. The choices you make will change your outcome. After you finish one path, go back and read the others for new perspectives and more adventures.

*YOU CHOOSE the path
you take through history.*

In 1912, *Titanic* was the world's largest ocean liner. The ship was 269 metres (882 feet, 9 inches) long.

CHAPTER 1

All aboard!

The year is 1912. A giant ship gleams in England's Southampton harbour. *Titanic's* looming shadow makes even the most powerful passenger feel small. No ship this big has ever been built.

The huge ship was built with safety in mind. Watertight walls called bulkheads are designed to keep water from flowing from one part of the ship to another. The ship also has 15 watertight doors. Newspapers say that *Titanic* is "practically unsinkable".

7

Turn the page.

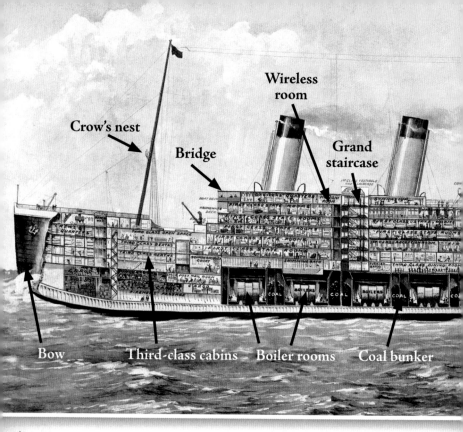

Crow's nest

Bridge

Wireless room

Grand staircase

Bow

Third-class cabins

Boiler rooms

Coal bunker

All over the world, people await *Titanic*'s first voyage with excitement. They've followed the newspaper stories about it for months. It took three years to build *Titanic*, at a cost of £1.5 million. The ship has a saltwater swimming pool, a library, a gym, and three elevators.

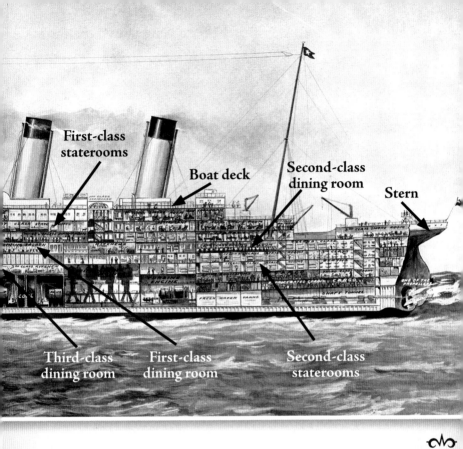

First-class
staterooms

Boat deck

Second-class
dining room

Stern

Third-class
dining room

First-class
dining room

Second-class
staterooms

In all, 1,316 passengers will travel aboard *Titanic* across the Atlantic Ocean to New York City. Some of the world's richest people have planned for months to take this first voyage. They have paid thousands of pounds for the trip.

Turn the page.

But the rich aren't the only ones to experience this amazing ship. Third-class passengers step on a wooden gangway into the lower levels of the ship. Many are immigrants from Europe seeking a better life in the United States.

Some people travelling on the ship aren't passengers. The ship has a crew of 890 people. They include cooks, stewards, engineers, and a doctor. Other staff members work for private companies. These people are orchestra members, wireless radio operators, and restaurant workers.

Captain Edward Smith led the ship's crew of 890 people.

• *To travel with the rich in first class, turn to page* **13**.

• *To travel with the poor in third class,*
turn to page **47**.

• *To travel as a crewmember, turn to page* **73**.

The grand staircase connected the first-class areas of the ship.

CHAPTER 2

A first-class experience

As you step on *Titanic*'s deck, the chief steward welcomes you aboard. Another steward leads you to your stateroom.

Your stateroom is as elegant as a grand hotel. Carved oak lines the walls. Some mirrors are trimmed in gold. Every stateroom has electric light and heat. It makes you feel like royalty.

Once you've settled in, you decide to explore the ship. You spot the ship's grand staircase. Topped by an iron and glass dome, it is dazzling.

Turn the page.

Around noon, you walk up near the bridge. Captain Edward Smith is there, directing the officers, quartermasters, and pilot. You hear the officers at their stations signal that they are ready. The pilot calls out, "Let go the hold ropes!" Crewmembers relay the orders. Tugboats help the great ship inch out of the harbour.

As the ship heads out to sea, you move to the first-class lounge. There, you meet two wealthy, famous men. John Jacob Astor and Hudson Allison are returning home on *Titanic*.

Astor is an old friend. You haven't seen him since he left for Europe four months ago with his new bride. This Allison fellow seems interesting, too. He speaks with pride of his two young children, who are also aboard. Separately, both men invite you to join them a few nights later for dinner.

Titanic's reading and writing room was as elegant as a room in an expensive hotel.

‣ *To join Allison, turn to page* **17.**

‣ *To join Astor, turn to page* **20.**

Hudson Allison was returning to Canada from a horse-buying trip in England.

It is Sunday, 14 April, your fifth night on *Titanic*. You join the Allisons for dinner in the first-class dining room. Hudson Allison introduces you to his wife, Bess, and 2-year-old daughter, Loraine. Normally, children aren't present in the dining room, but Mrs Allison wanted Loraine to see the beautiful room.

A few minutes later, the Allisons' maids, Alice Cleaver and Sarah Daniels, walk up to the table. Alice holds the Allisons' baby son, Trevor. Sarah takes Loraine's hand, and the women leave to put the children to bed.

Also at the table are two of Hudson Allison's friends from Canada, Harry Molson and Arthur Peuchen. Soon, the talk turns to the *Titanic*.

Turn the page.

"I've crossed the ocean 40 times, but never quite as comfortably as on this ship," Peuchen says. "There's only one thing that worries me."

"What's that?" you ask.

"I'm not sure that Captain Smith is up to the job," he replies. "He's too old, and his record isn't spotless. I don't know if I'd trust him with my life."

"Don't worry, my friend," Hudson Allison says to Peuchen. "The journey has gone well so far. In a few days, you'll be home with your family."

After a delicious meal and several hours of conversation, it is time for the night to end. You shake hands with the other men and head to your stateroom. You quickly dress for bed and fall asleep.

Suddenly, someone knocks loudly on your stateroom door. How long have you been asleep? Your watch says it's midnight – just one hour. The steward at your door calls out, "I'm sorry to inform you that the captain has ordered all on deck with life jackets."

• *To take the warning seriously and leave your room, turn to page 22.*

• *To stay in your room, turn to page 26.*

Madeleine and John Jacob Astor were returning from their honeymoon.

On Sunday, 14 April, you arrive for dinner with the Astors. John Jacob Astor greets you in the entryway to the dining room. He is dressed neatly in a tuxedo, and his beautiful young bride is wearing an elegant dress.

As you sit down to dinner, Astor entertains you and the others at the table with tales of his business deals in New York and in Europe. It is a fun, festive night. You all eat your fill.

After dinner, you and the other men move to the smoking room. You spend the next few hours playing cards before returning to your stateroom.

As you get ready for bed, there is a pounding on your door. A steward calls, "I'm sorry to inform you that the captain has ordered all on deck with life jackets."

What's this? Is it a drill, or a serious problem? You aren't sure what to do. Suddenly, you think of the Astors. If there is trouble, they should be warned.

• *To go to warn the Astors, turn to page 33.*

• *To follow the instructions and head out on deck, turn to page 34.*

You dash around your room, trying to decide what to bring. You grab your life jacket, a heavy coat, and £40. You follow the steward towards the boat deck. People stumble out of staterooms, whispering about what might be the trouble. You realize that the rumble you've grown used to is no longer there – *Titanic*'s engines have stopped.

On the boat deck, the atmosphere is calm. The man next to you says, "All this trouble for nothing, I'm sure. Nothing can sink *Titanic*." The crew begins filling a few lifeboats with passengers. Several crewmembers are calling out, "Women and children first!"

You hear a couple of crewmembers talking. "Earlier tonight we received a warning of ice in the area," one of them says. "Sure enough, we've struck ice."

You peer over the railing to the decks below. There, young people are playing with chunks of ice that have landed on deck. Some passengers cheer them on, but you feel uneasy.

You move back along the deck. There, you see Sarah Daniels, the Allisons' maid. You call to her, and she rushes over to you.

Sarah explains that she had awakened the Allisons to tell them to come to the deck. Instead, they became angry with her for waking them. Sarah then left to investigate. Now, she was being forced into a lifeboat.

"It's just a precaution, ma'am," a crewmember says. Then he whisks Sarah into lifeboat number 8.

Turn the page.

On its boat deck, *Titanic* carried 16 wooden lifeboats and four collapsible lifeboats.

You glance down the railing at the other lifeboats. Most hold a few passengers, but many of the first-class passengers don't want to leave *Titanic*.

You quickly count the lifeboats. There doesn't appear to be enough of them for all the passengers and crew aboard. Even worse, the ones that are being lowered aren't close to being full.

The crew launches rockets into the black sky to alert other ships. As Sarah's half-full lifeboat is lowered, she calls to you. "Please, sir, find Mr and Mrs Allison. They need to know they're in danger!"

• *To find out more about the lifeboat situation, turn to page* **28**.

• *To search for the Allisons, turn to page* **29**.

Startled, you sit up straight. "What's that?" you yell into the darkness. There is no response. You tiptoe to the door and open it a crack. Passengers are leaving their rooms, some still in their nightclothes. Most of them are unhappy. "I don't see why we should take part in your lifeboat drill," one woman complains.

You close your door. You will not be bothered with any boat drills, either.

Later, another noise jars you from your sleep. It feels like a thud or a crack.

Stepping out of bed, you slide on your slippers and pull on a robe. Remembering the steward's call, you grab a life jacket. You crack open the door to the lit passageway. It is empty. You have no idea what's happened, but you know you need to get up on deck.

Titanic's bow and bridge went underwater first.

The view from the second-highest deck is frightening. Under the moonless sky, tiny boats row away. Crewmembers scramble about. You move to the rail.

You look to the boat deck above you, but all the lifeboats are gone. Ropes hang from the side of the ship. The deck tilts forward at an odd angle. Suddenly, you feel the ship lurch up. Screams come from the decks above and below you. You have only one choice now.

Turn to page **44**.

Crewmembers are lowering lifeboats on both sides of the ship. You make your way to the starboard, or right, side of the deck. There, an officer is directing a group of passengers into a half-filled boat.

"Sir!" the officer calls to you. "We have room for one more!"

"Shouldn't we wait to see if there are more women and children onboard?" you ask him.

"My instructions are to lower this boat," he replies. "If you want a seat, take it now."

Reluctantly, you step into the boat.

Turn to page 42.

More people crowd the decks. As crewmembers continue to call for women and children, some men also take seats in the lifeboats. Meanwhile, some women refuse to leave their husbands behind. Some male passengers lift women into the boats. You see one panicked woman screaming and fighting the men. She then breaks away and runs back inside the ship.

As you head for the Allisons' stateroom, you spot Alice Cleaver. She is near the ship's edge, holding baby Trevor. You call to her, but she can't hear you over the growing noise on the deck. It is getting harder to walk on the deck now, because the ship is tilting forward.

· To run to Alice and Trevor, turn to page **30**.

· To continue to look for the Allisons, turn to page **32**.

Bess and Loraine Allison became separated from baby Trevor during the disaster.

You fight your way through the crowd to Alice and Trevor. By the time you reach them, Alice is stepping into a lifeboat. She holds Trevor in her arms. She sees you and calls your name. "Come quickly!" she says. "*Titanic* is sinking!"

You climb into the boat and sit next to Alice. She clutches Trevor to her chest. Instantly, the lifeboat is lowered towards the icy waters of the Atlantic. You can feel the water's chill in your bones as you get nearer to it.

When the lifeboat touches the ocean, you and the other men aboard grab oars. You try to row away from the ship as fast as possible. The crewmember commanding the lifeboat urges you on, as he also rows. "We must get away, or we'll be pulled down with her!" he yells.

Suddenly, you hear a loud noise. It appears *Titanic* has split in two. The great ship is headed for the ocean floor.

Turn to page **36**.

The crowd of people coming out to the deck is getting steady now. It is growing harder to get back inside. You worry that you won't reach the Allisons in time. You get swept up in the crowd, and end up on the other side of the ship.

You spot the Allisons. Mrs Allison is holding Loraine's hand as they board a lifeboat. Hudson remains on deck.

Before the lifeboat can be lowered, though, Mrs Allison fights her way to the edge. Clutching Loraine to her, she climbs back onto the deck. "I will not leave without my baby!" she cries. The family then heads off towards the other side of the ship. You follow, hoping that you can lead them to where you saw Alice and Trevor.

Turn to page 38.

You grab your life jacket and leave your stateroom. When you finally find the Astors, they are in the gym. They greet you as you walk in, but there's little time to talk. A crewmember calls into the room, urging everyone to go up on deck.

On deck, a crewmember tells you that all the lifeboats are being loaded. Astor doesn't believe the passengers are in serious danger. "I'm sure we'll be fine aboard the big ship," he says. It doesn't matter, as the crew is loading women and children first.

Mrs Astor isn't sure that boarding a lifeboat is a good idea. But her husband asks her to get on the boat as a precaution. As her lifeboat is lowered, he calls to her, "We'll meet in New York!"

Turn to page 39.

You grab your life jacket and strap it on quickly. You also put on warm socks, trousers, and a sturdy pair of shoes. Whatever's happened, this doesn't seem like a time to be dressed for dinner. It feels more like your training as a yachtsman might come in handy.

On deck, crewmembers are scrambling around to prepare lifeboats. There are a few passengers on deck, but many are not wearing their life jackets. You grab a crewmember as he goes by. "Is this a drill?" you ask. "No, sir," the crewmember says. His eyes tell you there is trouble. "I assure you it is not a drill."

You move over near the lifeboats and offer your help. "I'm a skilled sailor," you tell the crewmember working there. "Good," he replies. "We can use all the help we can get."

Cables and ropes helped lower the lifeboats to the sea.

You calm worried passengers and help them into boats. You help an officer prepare to lower one of the boats. Just then, the officer realizes there isn't a crewmember nearby.

Turn to page 40.

Titanic's end is painful to watch. Husbands call out to their wives in lifeboats. Some men leap for the water, hoping to swim to safety. Others stand calmly and await their fate as *Titanic's* stern lifts higher into the air. Then, what is left of the great ship disappears into the Atlantic. All you can do now is to wait and hope for a rescue. You shiver against the cold night air.

As you wait, an argument brews on your lifeboat. Some want to row back towards the spot where *Titanic* sank to look for survivors. Others disagree. "There's not a person alive in these icy waters," one man says.

Soon, you all notice the silence around you. There are no more calls for help. There is no point in going back.

Survivors moved their boats together as the ship sank.

About 4 o'clock in the morning, the steamer *Carpathia* arrives. You are one of 705 people to survive the sinking of *Titanic*. More than 1,500 others are not so lucky.

THE END

To follow another path, turn to page 11.
To read the conclusion, turn to page 101.

Panic grows on deck. The bow of the ship steadily sinks beneath the water's surface. Everyone runs for the ship's stern to escape. You fight to keep your balance as the stern rises until it is almost straight up in the air.

Suddenly, you hear a loud noise. The ship is breaking in two! As the decks turn upright, you cling to the railing. All around you, people lose their grip and fall into the frozen waters far below.

There is no safety for you and the Allisons now. All that lies ahead is the icy waters of the Atlantic Ocean. As the giant ocean liner sinks, you catch the eye of another passenger. It is the last sight you will ever see.

THE END

To follow another path, turn to page 11.
To read the conclusion, turn to page 101.

You stand near Astor and watch as boat after boat is loaded. Soon, it becomes clear that there aren't enough lifeboats for all the passengers. Unless a rescue ship arrives quickly, you, Astor, and many others will go down with *Titanic*.

As the final lifeboats are lowered, sounds swirl around you. Husbands and wives call to each other. The ship's band continues to play ragtime music, then changes to a hymn.

In the confusion, you make one last decision. You return to your stateroom. You take in the luxury all around you, knowing that your fate is sealed.

THE END

To follow another path, turn to page 11.
To read the conclusion, turn to page 101.

The officer turns to you. "Can you command a boat, sir?" he asks. You nod. The officer motions for you to board the boat. Within minutes, your boat is lowered down the side of *Titanic*. You begin to row away from the ship as quickly as possible. The women and children in the boat sob quietly.

Many of them have left loved ones aboard *Titanic*. And the farther you row, the more it becomes clear that *Titanic* is headed for a watery grave. You move your boat close to the other lifeboats drifting by.

The crew of *Carpathia* rescued *Titanic* survivors on the morning of 15 April.

Two hours later, another passenger spies the lights of the steamer *Carpathia*. You and the people you helped are saved.

THE END

To follow another path, turn to page 11.
To read the conclusion, turn to page 101.

Lifeboats were lowered 23 metres (75 feet) from the boat deck.

75 FEET FROM BOAT DECK TO WATER.

As your boat is lowered about 23 metres (75 feet) to the water, you look around. Your boat is among the first to reach the Atlantic. A crewmember rows you away from the giant ocean liner.

From a distance, you watch the horrible sight as *Titanic*'s bow disappears underwater. The stern is almost straight up in the air.

Screams tear through the air as people still aboard jump to escape the doomed ship. After what seems like forever, the lights of the ship go out. All is silent.

The crewmember turns your lifeboat around and rows back towards the spot where *Titanic* once floated. Together, you search the area for survivors.

Most of the bodies in the water are frozen and lifeless. But you do find a few people still alive. You help them into the boat and keep them warm until help arrives.

THE END

To follow another path, turn to page 11.
To read the conclusion, turn to page 101.

You strap the life jacket around your chest. You pause for a moment and take a deep breath. Finally, you jump.

It seems like forever before you strike the freezing water. When you do, the shock takes your breath away. You plunge deep into the water. You swim hard for the surface, struggling to hold your breath.

At last, you break into the cold night air, gasping for breath. You swim with all your might away from *Titanic*.

44

The cold water quickly takes away your strength. No lifeboats are nearby. As the mighty ship sinks, you cling to a floating piece of wood. But you can't stop shaking, and you know you won't last long in the icy water.

Suddenly, you see a light flashing over the water. "Is anyone there?" a man calls.

"I'm over here!" you croak with the last of your strength. The lifeboat rows over and pulls you aboard. Just when it seemed all hope was lost, you are rescued.

THE END

To follow another path, turn to page 11.
To read the conclusion, turn to page 101.

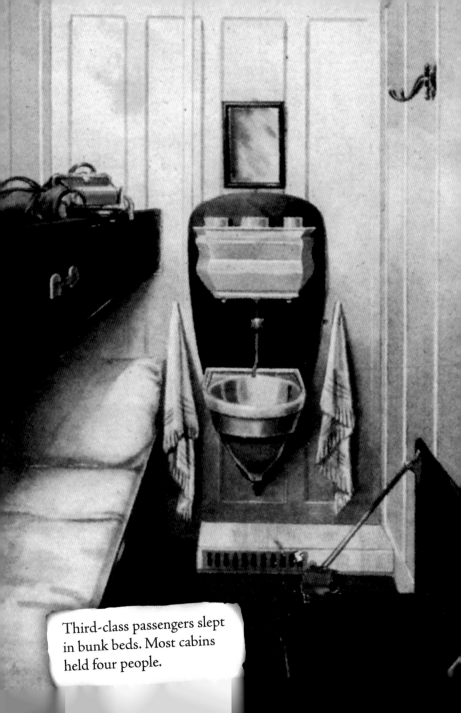

Third-class passengers slept in bunk beds. Most cabins held four people.

CHAPTER 3

On the way to the United States

Finally, your long wait is over. You have wished for a chance to go to the United States to start a new life. Now, your time has come.

After buying your ticket, you have to pass a medical inspection. You wait in a long line to be checked for trachoma and other diseases. Once you pass the inspection, you receive your boarding papers and step aboard *Titanic*.

While you've never travelled on an ocean liner before, you have heard stories about the poor conditions in third class. But on *Titanic*, even third class is clean and comfortable.

Turn the page.

Third-class passengers weren't allowed on the boat deck.

You hear one woman say, "This is like travelling in second class on most ships."

You've been assigned to a cabin on one of the lower decks. As you enter it, you see that you'll be sharing the cosy room with three other women. There are two bunk beds and a small sink in the room. You place your belongings on one of the bunks and take a deep breath.

Outside, hundreds of people move through the narrow passageways. They speak many languages. Some of it you understand, and some of it you don't. But it doesn't really matter to you. The greatest adventure of your life is about to begin.

· If you are an English-speaking passenger, turn to page **50**.

· If you do not speak English, turn to page **52**.

At noon, the ship finally sets sail. All around you, people celebrate. New York is only a few short days away.

Even though you are travelling alone, you never feel lonely. You get to know your three bunkmates quickly. They are also hoping for a better life in the United States.

Mealtimes are always fun. The food is better than what you usually eat at home. Soups, stews, roast pork, boiled potatoes, and fresh bread are all plentiful.

The third-class dining room was decorated simply but comfortably.

Night-time is when the real fun begins, however. After dinner, passengers gather in the general room for music, dancing, and singing.

It is Sunday, 14 April, your fifth night on the ship. You attended church services in the morning and later enjoyed a fine meal in the dining room. As fun as the trip has been, you are beginning to feel tired and restless after so many days at sea.

It feels like this might be a good night to go to bed early. But before you can leave, a man you met the night before approaches your table. His name is Tony. He invites you and your friends to the general room.

• To go the general room with Tony and your friends, turn to page 54.

• To return to your cabin for the night, turn to page 55.

As you wait for the ship to sail, you make yourself comfortable in your room. Two of your cabin mates arrive. They are speaking a language you don't understand. You try to communicate with them, but it is hard.

Still, you continue trying. They seem like nice women. After a short while, they leave the cabin. You wait, thinking about what your voyage will be like.

Later, your third cabin mate arrives. When she walks in the door, she looks a little frightened. You rise from your bunk and greet her. With that, a huge grin spreads across her face. She responds in your language, and you both feel better.

You talk about your excitement to get to the United States. You are both nervous about the trip. Like you, she's never travelled by ship before.

Still, the thought of a new life is enough to calm your worries. Your new friend invites you to stay with her family in New York City when you arrive.

The first few days of the trip are filled with new discoveries, adventures, and fun. The meals are better than you get at home. The nights are full of music, singing, and dancing in the general room.

On Sunday night, you decide to go to bed early. Late that night, a jolt wakes you. You notice that the vibration of the ship's engines is gone. Should you leave your room to investigate?

· To leave your room and investigate, turn to page **61**.

· To go back to sleep, turn to page **63**.

Since it is Sunday, there is no loud music or dancing in the general room. But a few passengers have brought musical instruments. They lead the others in singing hymns. You add your voice to the harmony.

As the night grows late, though, something strange happens. You feel a jolt that causes you to slightly lose your balance. You glance at the other passengers. Some seem to have noticed it. Others keep right on singing.

For the next few minutes, you ask people if they noticed anything. Some say they have, but others say they haven't. You are worried. The vibration of the ship's movement is gone.

54

· To leave the general room to investigate, turn to page **56**.

· To stay, turn to page **58**.

You move through the passageways back towards your cabin. When you open the door, you see you are alone. You smile, knowing that a quiet room means sleep will come quickly.

You change into your nightgown and slide beneath the blankets. After a few moments, you are fast asleep.

· *Turn to page* **70**.

You fight your way through the crowd in the general room. When you reach the passageway, you head towards your cabin. People are talking, but no one seems very concerned. Finally, you see a steward. "Remain calm," he says. "Return to your cabins and find your life jackets."

You're too worried to return to your room. You go to find a stairway to the upper decks. When you reach one, you have another reason to worry. At the top of the steps, several people lean against a metal gate. The gate separates third-class quarters from the first- and second-class rooms. As usual, it is locked.

You climb the steps to find out what is going on. "The ship hit an iceberg," one person says. "People are getting into lifeboats. But we can't get past this gate."

You feel your dream slipping away. You are not going to let that happen. You ask the men who are standing near the gate to help you. Together, you force your way through it, breaking the lock.

Stewards warned passengers to wear their life jackets after the ship struck ice.

‣ *Turn to page 64.*

The singing continues in the general room. The temperature in the room is rising.

As time passes, you notice the crowd thinning. More and more people have left the room, and they have not returned. The music finally dies down, and you notice something odd. The room appears to be tipping to one side. You wonder if there is a serious problem.

When you walk into the passageway, it is filled with passengers. Some of them are wearing their life jackets. "What's happened?" you ask. The answer worries you even more: *Titanic* has struck ice. "We've been told to stay below decks," the man says. "They will tell us when it's time for us to go up." This answer is not good enough for you.

You head to the stairwell that leads to the upper decks of the ship. There is a crowd of people there, but they aren't moving. They are stuck behind a locked metal gate. Some of them are pleading with a steward to unlock the gate. You work your way through the crowd until you reach the gate. The steward looks nervous as he unfastens the lock.

• *Turn to page 66.*

Passengers gathered
on the boat deck after the
ship struck an iceberg.

You step out into the passageway. A few other passengers are also there. You don't understand what most of them are saying. You decide to head up to a higher deck.

When you reach the deck, you see a strange sight. There are chunks of ice all around. Some of them are bigger than your head. Children are playing a game with them. You wonder if this situation could be serious.

The crewmembers seem to be telling people to return to their cabins. There are many passengers on deck, some of them in their nightclothes.

You rush back towards your cabin to wake your friend. As you fight your way back to the lower decks, you face a tide of people heading in the other direction.

Turn the page.

The situation is worse by the time you reach the deck where your cabin is located. Water is ankle-deep on the floors, and people are starting to panic. You reach your cabin, but it is empty. Your friend must have got out. Now, you realize you are on your own. You need to get back to the upper decks.

You head towards the back of the ship. There, you find some people who have discovered a ladder that leads up a hatch to the boat deck. As you reach the boat deck, however, you learn horrible news. All of the lifeboats have been lowered.

‹ *Turn to page* **68**.

You raise your head off your pillow. You can hear a few people talking out in the passageway, but you can't understand what they are saying. It sounds like a normal conversation to you, so you do your best to ignore it. It's been a long few days. The trip has left you tired. Sleep will come quickly.

• *Turn to page* **70.**

Up on deck, you make your way to the port, or left, side. Most passengers are wearing life jackets, and many of them are in their nightclothes. Suddenly, it's hard to tell the first-class passengers from the second- and third-class passengers.

Crewmembers are leading women and children into lifeboats, but men are being told to wait. Some women refuse to leave their husbands, but most are getting into the boats.

Near the deck railing, you spot Tony. You ask him what he is doing.

"I'm trying to decide what to do," he answers. "They won't let me board a lifeboat. Should I jump?"

You think briefly about the situation. "No, don't jump," you reply. "You'll freeze in that water."

A crewmember asks Tony to step back from the edge of the ship, but he refuses. He seems to have made his decision. Just as a lifeboat is about to be lowered, Tony grabs you by the hand. He leaps into the lifeboat, pulling you along with him. The crewmember orders Tony out of the lifeboat. Again, he refuses.

Finally, the crewmember pulls a gun from his coat. He fires a warning shot into the air. "Return to the ship!" he shouts. But you realize that he doesn't have the heart to pull Tony off the lifeboat. As the lifeboat reaches the water below, you know that your dream is still alive.

THE END

To follow another path, turn to page 11.
To read the conclusion, turn to page 101.

As the gate opens, passengers stream through it. Up on deck, passengers and crewmembers are moving about quickly. Still, no one seems to be panicking.

You hear a crewmember call, "Women and children first!" as people board the lifeboats. You worry that only first-class passengers will be allowed in the boats. But now is no time to be cautious.

"Miss!" a crewmember calls to you. "Get aboard!" You step into the lifeboat and sit down. You let out a big sigh of relief.

The boat is lowered towards the water. Some of the women in the boat with you sob silently. Others call out to the men on deck. "We'll meet in New York!" one man yells from the deck.

Titanic's electric lights blazed until the ship disappeared beneath the ocean's surface.

As the crewmember aboard the lifeboat rows away from *Titanic*, you see that the man's hope is unlikely. The ship is sinking. But you and the others in your boat are safe. You'll be among those rescued later that morning.

THE END

To follow another path, turn to page 11.
To read the conclusion, turn to page 101.

People on deck are screaming. Some call out to loved ones on lifeboats. Suddenly, you hear a huge crack. The ship lurches forwards, and you lose your balance. The deck is slanted now, and you slowly slide down it. You reach out and catch a rope. You cling to it tightly.

Others are not so lucky. As the deck tilts higher, they slide, trying desperately to grab anything they can. Most of them slide off. You wrap yourself in the rope, hoping it can somehow save you. But *Titanic's* bow keeps slipping lower and lower into the ocean.

You cling tightly to the rope until the last minute. As the water rises up, you release the rope. You drop into the icy water. The suction created by the sinking ship pulls you down. You desperately swim for the surface. Finally, your head breaks above the water.

You swim towards the lifeboats. The freezing water seems to squeeze your lungs. You reach a collapsible lifeboat with a few people in it. As you reach the boat, no one reaches out to help you. "Don't capsize us!" one person yells. Slowly, you pull yourself in and wait for the rescue ship. Your journey to the United States turned out to be much more than you could ever have imagined.

The collapsible lifeboats were the last to be launched.

THE END

To follow another path, turn to page 11.
To read the conclusion, turn to page 101.

Suddenly, you awaken. There's a chill in your room, and you can hear panicked voices outside. Some people are screaming. You can't see anything in the dark room. But as you turn to stand, you realize that water covers the floor.

You run to the door. The water is nearly knee-deep. Can it be? Can *Titanic* be sinking? You pull the door open to see a passageway packed with frightened people.

As you move into the passageway, the ship lurches. Some people lose their balance. They scream as they slip into the water. Others stay up and keep moving forward. You do your best to help people to their feet. But then the boat tilts again, and more people fall.

As the passageway tilts, it becomes clear that you will not make it to the upper decks. Soon, you are hanging onto a door frame while others around you slip and fall, hitting walls and other people as they go. You feel your grip loosen. As you fall through the passageway, your head smacks against a wall. Everything goes dark.

You are unconscious. And as *Titanic* plunges to the ocean floor, you are taken down with it. You will never know how or why the great ship sank.

THE END

To follow another path, turn to page 11.
To read the conclusion, turn to page 101.

Titanic set sail at about noon on 10 April.

CHAPTER 4

To protect and serve

As the sun rises on 10 April, you make your way to Southampton's harbour. As you board *Titanic*, you see some familiar faces among the other crewmembers. You see stewards, who attend to the needs of the passengers. Also in the crowd are cooks, musicians, and engine room workers, called stokers.

Over the years, you've worked on many ships. But you've never been on one this grand. You're excited to see how the ship feels in the open water. You've heard promises that *Titanic's* ride will be smooth. You can't wait to see if the stories are true.

Turn the page.

As the passengers board, you prepare for a long week of work. After all, in order for the passengers to enjoy their adventure, you've got to keep things moving.

Finally, it's time to set sail. The gangplanks are pulled in, and the ship is ready to move out to sea.

• *To work as a member of the deck crew, go to page 75.*

• *To work on the engine crew, turn to page 76.*

The mood of this voyage is different from any you've ever been on. Passengers arrive with broad smiles and few demands. All around, you hear people talking about the beauty of *Titanic*.

Even in third class, passengers are excited to be on their way. Most of them seem to be off to start a new life in the United States. They are pleased to find out that they have comfortable rooms and plenty of food.

• *To work with the deck crew as a junior officer, turn to page 82.*

• *To work below deck as a third-class steward, turn to page 83.*

As the ship leaves the harbour, your watch is just beginning. You step into one of the boiler rooms, which hold the coal-burning furnaces that supply power to the ship's engines. You take your spot with the other stokers.

You work in the deep, dark belly of *Titanic* as you stoke the boilers. You feel their heat with every shovelful of coal. Every 7 minutes, a gong sounds to tell you it is time to shovel more coal. Dials on the boilers show you which boiler needs coal next.

Titanic's ride does not feel as smooth to you as it does to the passengers above. But you can tell from the vibrations in the floor that the engines are working properly.

In 1912, coal supplied the power for most ships.

Turn the page.

Everything isn't perfect, though. Right after you start your first watch, you learn about a fire aboard the ship. The fire broke out in boiler room 6 a week earlier, while the ship was still in port. The stokers in that room have worked ever since to put out the fire, but it is still smouldering.

On the fifth night, you report for work at your usual time. The good news is that the fire in boiler room 6 is finally out. You hope this means that the rest of the trip will go smoothly.

Suddenly, a red light flashes in your boiler compartment. Someone yells, "Shut all the dampers!"

In an instant, a huge crash sends you flying. You bounce off the steel wall behind you. The other stokers are also flung about the boiler room. The sounds of the ship have changed. The roar of the huge engines is replaced by the sound of rushing water.

A few of the other stokers appear to be hurt. In the distance, you hear the sound of watertight doors slamming shut. You have only a split second to decide what to do next.

• *To go immediately to the emergency exit, turn to page 80.*

• *To help the injured workers, turn to page 96.*

One of the nearby watertight doors is still open. Water has begun rushing into your compartment. There's no time to waste.

You dive for the door. You slide through to the other side. Two or three others make it through before the heavy metal door slams shut. You can hear your fellow stokers pounding on the other side. But it's too late to help them.

You quickly climb the emergency exit ladder. You pry open the hatch and climb up to the deck above.

Soon, you see an officer. He tells you what has happened – *Titanic* has struck ice. The huge liner is sinking. He orders you to get into a nearby lifeboat. Its passengers will need a strong man to row them away.

Stokers who made it out waited to see if they would be allowed in the lifeboats.

• *Turn to page 97.*

You've spent your life travelling the oceans, working on all types of ships. You've worked hard to reach the position of officer, and are pleased to be hired for *Titanic*'s first voyage.

During the first days of the voyage, you work steadily. You supervise other crewmembers and watch the ocean and the skies for anything that might endanger the ship. You know most of the crewmembers. Many of you have worked together on other ships.

Finally, Sunday arrives. It's your night off. You're looking forward to relaxing, but your best friend is working on the bridge tonight. He's asked you to stop by to help in case things get busy.

· *To take the night off, turn to page* **86**.

· *To go to the bridge to find your friend, turn to page* **88**.

You were disappointed when you first learned you would be working in third class. Like most stewards, you would rather work in first class, where the big tips make up for the long hours and demanding passengers. But now, you find you're enjoying working in third class on *Titanic*. Many of the passengers work as servants themselves. They are thrilled to have someone waiting on them.

It is Sunday, 14 April, and your watch is just ending. You're ready to have some fun with your fellow crewmembers. But on your way to meet your friends, something rocks the ship. You go to the deck to find out what's happened.

On deck, you hear the bad news: *Titanic* has struck an iceberg and is taking on water. You must go back to third class to warn the passengers.

Turn the page.

The huge iceberg shattered as *Titanic* struck it.

As you reach the locked gates that separate third class from first and second class, you see a group of panicked passengers behind a gate. They're worried they will be trapped below the decks. You grab your keys and unlock the gate. The passengers stream through.

You unlock a few more gates and help passengers find life jackets. But you know that your job isn't done. On the boat deck, passengers are being loaded into lifeboats. If needed, you will board and command one of the lifeboats as it launches.

As you hurry up to the boat deck, you pass by the wireless room. The wireless operators might also need some help. What should you do?

· To continue to the boat deck, turn to page **91**.

· To go into the wireless room, turn to page **94**.

You return to your sleeping quarters. After several long days of work, you can finally take care of some personal matters. You write letters to your family back home in England. You tell about the people you've met. You brag about the wonderful ship you are working on.

It's getting close to midnight. The hum of the ship's gigantic engines calms you. You feel ready for sleep.

But just as you rest your head on the pillow, you feel the ship turn oddly. Your experience tells you there was an abrupt change of course. You rise from your bed just in time to feel a strange sensation. It feels like *Titanic* has run over a bed of marbles.

You know something isn't right. You dress quickly and leave your cabin to find out what has happened. On the way out, you grab your gun – just in case.

• *To go to the starboard side of the boat deck, turn to page 90.*

• *To go to the port side of the boat deck, turn to page 92.*

It's very late, and the night is cold and dark. No moon shines overhead to cast a sparkle across the smooth ocean. We should be able to make good time tonight, you think.

Before you get to the bridge, however, something startles you. It's a call from the crow's nest up above. "Iceberg! Right ahead!" You hear the panic in the lookout's voice. But deep down, you aren't worried. Surely, *Titanic* will steer away from it.

The great ship begins a gentle turn. You move quickly to the railing and look into the distance. Squinting, you finally see the iceberg.

You watch as *Titanic* veers slightly to the left. But it's too late. *Titanic*'s starboard side glances off the iceberg. The collision throws you off balance for a moment. Chunks of ice land on the deck around you.

The iceberg *Titanic* struck was about 30 metres (100 feet) tall.

Was the collision enough to damage the ship? You realize that you need to find someone who can tell you exactly what is going on.

- *To rush to the boat deck, turn to page* **92**.
- *To head to the wireless room, turn to page* **94**.

As you reach the starboard side of the boat deck, you see the ship's first officer, William Murdoch, uncovering the lifeboats.

"What's happened, sir?" you ask.

"We've struck an iceberg," Murdoch replies. "Captain Smith has issued the call of distress. I need you to help load passengers into the lifeboats."

You gulp, knowing the situation must be serious. Like the other crewmembers, though, you remain calm. There is some talk that the lights of a nearby ship can be seen. But one thing is clear – *Titanic* is in trouble.

Stewards, who are in charge of serving the passengers, head off to knock on cabin doors to wake passengers. They go to the first-class rooms, then second-class, and finally third.

As the sleepy passengers arrive on deck, many are annoyed. One man even exclaims, "You won't catch me in one of those little boats. We're much safer aboard the big ship." But you know better.

You encourage passengers to board the lifeboats. Following your training, you load women and children first. Some women refuse to leave their husbands. When the lifeboat is half full, you try to convince the remaining passengers to board. Again, they refuse. You are the last person to step into the boat.

Turn to page **97.**

As you reach the port side of the boat deck, you see Second Officer Charles Lightoller uncovering boats. You run to him and ask how you can help.

"Load the lifeboats with passengers," he replies. "Women and children first. Allow no men aboard the boats until the last woman and child has boarded. Do you understand me?" You nod.

During the next hour, passengers make their way to the deck. Some are angry. Others seem worried. But as *Titanic*'s bow starts to sink, people become frantic.

You follow Lightoller's orders and allow only women and children to board. As husbands separate from their wives and children, you sense the sadness of the moment.

Ship officers included Charles Lightoller (back row, second from left) and William Murdoch (front row, far right).

Some men try to get into the boats, and you do your best to stop them. In the background, you notice that the ship's band is playing. Maybe the music will help people stay calm.

Turn to page 98.

In the wireless room, the mood is calm. But you start to worry when Captain Smith walks into the room. He orders the operators to send out the call of distress.

Operator Jack Phillips sends out the call. The ship *Carpathia* replies that it is coming. But it is 93 kilometres (58 miles) away, and will take several hours to reach *Titanic*.

For the next 90 minutes, Phillips communicates with *Carpathia*. Every few minutes, you check on the conditions on deck. People are boarding lifeboats, which are being lowered to the sea. You help however you can.

Finally, Captain Smith walks into the wireless room. "Your work is done, boys," he says. "Look out for yourselves now."

Wireless operators on ships sent messages to the outside world.

You and the wireless operators look Captain Smith in the eye. You know he will go down with his ship. But he is giving you a chance of survival.

When you reach the deck, *Titanic* is nearly underwater, and all of the lifeboats are gone. There is only one hope – to jump.

Turn to page **99**.

You scramble to your feet and check on your crewmates. None of the injuries appear to be serious.

Water is rushing into your compartment. You all run for the door into the next compartment, but the huge watertight door is shutting. You find yourself at the back of the pack. One by one, several men escape through the door.

You will not be so lucky. The heavy door slams, leaving you and several other stokers trapped. You and the others beat on the steel door, but there is no answer from the other side. As the water rises, you stop pounding. You know there is no escape.

THE END

To follow another path, turn to page 11.
To read the conclusion, turn to page 101.

As the boat is lowered, you catch a glimpse of Captain Smith and salute him. You know you will never see him again.

After *Titanic* sinks, you row back. You find many frozen, lifeless bodies. But it lifts your spirits to find a couple of people who are still alive. You help them into the lifeboat and keep them warm until help arrives.

Only one lifeboat returned to the spot where the ship sank to search for survivors.

THE END

To follow another path, turn to page 11.
To read the conclusion, turn to page 101.

As you help women into a boat, a man moves close to the edge. "Step back, sir," you tell him. The man refuses. You call for the boat to be lowered. Just as it begins to descend, the man grabs a woman's hand. They both leap into the boat.

You call for the boat to stop. You insist that the man get out, but he again refuses. You pull out your gun and fire a warning shot into the air. "Return to the ship!" you shout.

You eyes meet, but you can't bring yourself to shoot the man. You order the boat to be lowered. You know that the man will live. And unless you are lucky enough to board one of the last lifeboats, you probably will not.

THE END

To follow another path, turn to page 11.
To read the conclusion, turn to page 101.

98

Quickly, you put on a life jacket and jump. The shock of the freezing water takes your breath away. You swim for the nearest lifeboat, a collapsible that has room to spare. But it's hundreds of feet away. With each stroke, you feel your strength failing.

Finally, you stop swimming. You try to yell for help, but no one is close enough. As you turn back towards *Titanic*, you see the stern rise up. People scream as they slide down the decks towards the water below. As *Titanic* disappears into the Atlantic, you take your last breath.

THE END

To follow another path, turn to page 11.
To read the conclusion, turn to page 101.

Wireless operator Harold Bride leaves *Carpathia* with his frozen feet in bandages.

CHAPTER 5

After the disaster

Only 705 people survived the sinking of *Titanic*. Their class of travel played an important part in whether passengers lived or died. In first class, about 60 per cent survived, compared with 40 per cent in second class and only 25 per cent in third class.

Third-class rooms were located farthest from the upper decks. Because of fear of disease, they were separated from the other classes by locked gates. Also, many people in third class didn't speak English, so they couldn't understand the warnings.

Titanic carried 20 lifeboats – four more than the law required at the time. Most of the lifeboats could hold about 65 people, but almost all were launched with far fewer passengers. At first, many people didn't believe the ship would sink and wouldn't get on the boats. Crewmembers worried that if they loaded too many people on the boats, they would capsize.

Women and children were supposed to be loaded into lifeboats first. But ship officers followed this rule differently. On the port side, the officer allowed no men on the boats except crewmembers to command the boats. But the officer on the starboard side allowed men to board if no women or children were nearby. Sadly, 55 children died – all but one from third class. However, a number of wealthy men also went down with the ship.

From the lifeboats, people watched helplessly as *Titanic* split in two and disappeared into the ocean. For at least 20 minutes, screams for help echoed around them.

Some passengers begged crewmembers to go back and pick up survivors, but most refused. They were afraid the lifeboats would be swamped with people and capsize. Only one boat went back, about an hour after the ship sank. It rescued four people, one of whom later died.

Second-class passengers Michel and Edmund Navratil survived the sinking. Their father did not.

No one knows exactly why *Titanic* sank – and took only 2 hours and 40 minutes to go down. But some events helped make the disaster worse.

There were other ships closer to *Titanic* than *Carpathia*. One of them, *Californian*, was only 19 miles away. But *Californian*'s wireless operator shut down his system at 11.35. The ship didn't receive *Titanic*'s call of distress. *Californian*'s crew saw the rockets fired from *Titanic*, but didn't understand that they were distress signals.

Both the US and British governments investigated the disaster. Their findings led to many safety improvements.

After the investigation, ships had to have 24-hour radio communications and enough lifeboats for all passengers. They had to hold lifeboat drills before each voyage. Also, the US Coast Guard formed an agency to watch for icebergs in the North Atlantic.

Today, aeroplanes have replaced ships as the most popular way to travel across the ocean. But people are still fascinated by the tragic story of *Titanic*. Even after 100 years, they imagine what life was like aboard the beautiful, doomed ship.

Time line

1908 – Construction of *Titanic* begins at the Harland and Wolff Shipyard in Belfast, Ireland.

January 1912 – Lifeboats are installed on *Titanic*. There are 20 in all, 16 wooden and four collapsible.

10 April 1912, 9.30–11.30 a.m. – Passengers board the ship in Southampton, England.

10 April, noon – *Titanic* begins its first voyage.

10–11 April – *Titanic* stops in Cherbourg, France, and Queenstown, Ireland. Passengers board and get off at these stops.

14 April, 11.40 p.m. – The lookout spots an iceberg straight ahead. *Titanic* strikes it on the starboard, or right, side of its bow.

15 April, midnight – Captain Smith gives the order to send out a wireless message calling for help.

12.05 a.m. – *Carpathia* receives *Titanic*'s call of distress and immediately heads towards the scene of the accident.

12.25 a.m. – Officers are given the order to lower the lifeboats and to begin loading them, women and children first.

12.45 a.m. – A rocket is fired to attract the attention of other ships that may be nearby. The first lifeboat is lowered with only 28 of the 65 places filled.

2.15 a.m. – The last lifeboat is launched. There are still more than 1,500 people left aboard.

2.20 a.m. – *Titanic* breaks in two and sinks. Passengers in the water freeze to death.

4.10 a.m. – *Carpathia* picks up the first lifeboat. Its crewmembers search the area for more than four hours as they pick up survivors. Just before 9 a.m., *Carpathia* leaves the area for New York with 705 survivors.

18 April, 9.00 p.m. – *Carpathia* arrives in New York.

19 April to 25 May 1912 – Ships from Halifax, Canada, sail to the site of the disaster to recover bodies. Only 330 are ever found.

1 September 1985 – Oceanographer Dr Robert Ballard and his crew find the wreck of *Titanic* about 3,810 metres (12,500 feet) below the ocean's surface.

OTHER PATHS TO EXPLORE

In this book, you've seen how the events surrounding the *Titanic* disaster look different from three points of view.

Perspectives on history are as varied as the people who lived it. You can explore other paths on your own to learn more about what happened. Seeing history from many points of view is an important part of understanding it.

Here are some ideas for other *Titanic* points of view to explore:

- ◆ Titanic's captain bravely decided to go down with the ship. What were the hours leading up to the sinking like for him?

- ◆ In New York, family and friends of passengers spent several days waiting for news of their loved ones. What were those days like for them?

- ◆ Some passengers survived, but their family members didn't. What was the experience like for those survivors?

READ MORE

The Story of the Titanic, Steve Noon (Dorling Kindersley, 2012)

Titanic (Discover More), Sean Callery (Scholastic, 2014)

Titanic (DK Eyewitness), Simon Adams (Dorling Kindersley, 2014)

Titanic, Melissa Stewart (National Geographic Society, 2012)

INTERNET SITES

Visit these sites for more information about the Titanic:

www.bbc.co.uk/cbbc/clips/p00r0xtb
This site has a video clip of an interview with a survivor of the Titanic.

channel.nationalgeographic.com/channel/titanic-100-years/

www.kidskonnect.com/subjectindex/16-educational/history/281-titanic.html

Glossary

bow – front end of a ship

bridge – navigation area of a ship

capsize – to turn over in the water

stateroom – first-class passenger's sleeping quarters on a ship

stern – back end of a ship

steward – ship's officer who is in charge of food and meals; a steward is also an attendant on a ship.

stoker – crewmember in charge of tending a ship's boilers

trachoma – contagious disease that can cause blindness

vibration – rapid, trembling motion

watch – period of time that a ship's crewmember is on duty

wireless message – communication that uses radio waves

BIBLIOGRAPHY

Bryceson, Dave. *The Titanic Disaster: As Reported in the British National Press April–July 1912.* New York: Norton, 1997.

Encylopedia Titanica
http://www.encyclopedia-titanica.org

Kuntz, Tom, ed. *The Titanic Disaster Hearings: The Official Transcripts of the 1912 Senate Investigation.* New York: Pocket Books, 1998.

Mowbray, Jay Henry, ed. *Sinking of the Titanic: Eyewitness Accounts.* Mineola, N.Y.: Dover, 1998.

The Titanic Historical Society and Museum
http://www.Titanichistoricalsociety.org

Winocour, Jack, ed. *The Story of the Titanic, as Told by Its Survivors.* New York: Dover, 1960.

INDEX

Californian, 104
Carpathia, 37, 41, 94, 100, 104, 107

first-class passengers
    Allison, Bess, 17, 30, 32
    Allison, Hudson, 14, 16, 17, 18, 32
    Allison, Loraine, 17, 30, 32
    Allison, Trevor, 17, 29, 30–31, 32
    Astor, John Jacob, 14, 20, 33, 39
    Astor, Madeleine, 20, 33
    Cleaver, Alice, 17, 29, 30–31, 32
    Daniels, Sarah, 17, 23, 25

officers
    Lightoller, Charles, 92, 93
    Murdoch, William, 90, 93
    Smith, Edward, 11, 14, 18, 90, 94–95, 97, 106

rescue, 37, 41, 107

second-class passengers, 101, 103

Southampton, England, 7, 73, 106
stewards, 13, 73, 83, 90
stokers, 73, 76, 81
survivors, 36, 37, 41, 43, 97, 101, 103, 107

third-class passengers, 10, 46, 47, 48, 50, 75, 83, 101
Titanic
    boiler rooms, 76, 77, 78–79, 80
    bridge, 14, 27
    cabins, 46, 48
    collision with iceberg, 84, 88–89, 106
    cost, 8
    departure, 14, 72, 74, 106
    dining rooms, 17, 50
    discovery of wreck, 107
    engines, 76
    lifeboats, 24, 35, 42, 69, 97, 102, 106
    sinking, 27, 36, 37, 38, 43, 44, 67, 103, 107
    size, 6
    staterooms, 13
    wireless room, 94–95